APR 14

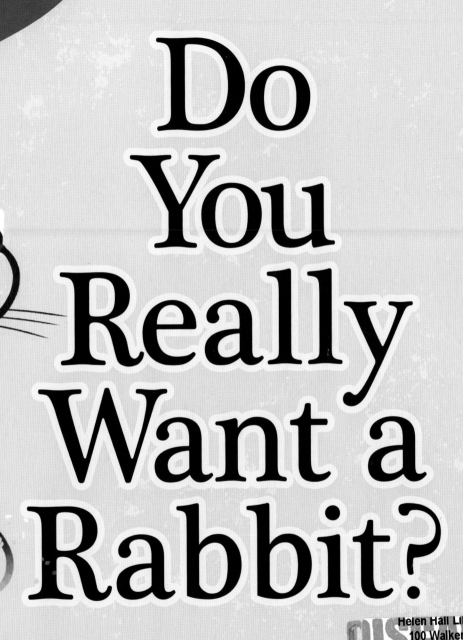

Do
You
Really
Want a
Rabbit?

Bridget Heos • Illustrated by Katya Longhi

Amicus Illustrated is published by Amicus
P.O. Box 1329, Mankato, MN 56002
www.amicuspublishing.us

Library of Congress Cataloging-in-Publication Data
Heos, Bridget.
 Do you really want a rabbit? / by Bridget Heos ; illustrated by Katya Longhi.
   pages cm. – (Do You Really Want a Pet?)
 Includes bibliographical references.
 Summary: "A shy, yet somewhat mischievous rabbit (and the narrator) teach a
young girl the responsibility–and the joys–of owning a rabbit. Includes 'Is this pet
right for me?' quiz"–Provided by publisher.
 ISBN 978-1-60753-208-8 (library binding) – ISBN 978-1-60753-400-6 (ebook)
 1. Rabbits–Juvenile literature. I. Longhi, Katya, illustrator. II. Title.
 SF453.2.H478 2014
 636.935–dc23
                         2012035937

Editor: Rebecca Glaser
Designer: The Design Lab

Printed in the United States of America at Corporate Graphics
in North Mankato, Minnesota.

Date 2/2013   PO 1146

10 9 8 7 6 5 4 3 2 1

About the Author

Bridget Heos is the author of more than
40 books for children and teens, including
What to Expect When You're Expecting Larvae
(2011, Lerner). She lives in Kansas City with
husband Justin, sons Johnny, Richie, and
J.J., plus a dog, cat, and Guinea pig.
You can visit her online at
www.authorbridgetheos.com.

About the Illustrator

Katya Longhi was born in southern Italy.
She studied illustration at the Nemo NT
Academy of Digital Arts in Florence. She loves
to create dream worlds with horses, flying
dogs, and princesses in her illustrations.
She currently lives in northern Italy
with her Prince Charming.

So you say you want a rabbit. You really, really want a rabbit.

But do you *really* want a rabbit?

You must let a rabbit get used to you.

If you don't…

. . . she'll be afraid. To her, you'll look like a big bad wolf! She'll scratch and bite to get away.

At first, let the bunny relax in her cage. The cage should have food, water, a bed, and a litter box.

After a few days, sit with her on the floor. Hold a treat, such as a carrot. Let her hop over. Pet her and speak softly. Do this every morning and evening. Eventually, she will let you hold her.

You're no longer a big bad wolf. You're a friend.
Now you can groom her. Comb her fur every week.

If you don't...

. . . she could get tangled! Bunnies help groom each other in the wild. Now, it's up to you. Just don't give her a bath. Bunnies bathe themselves. You'll still have to clean her cage once a week though.

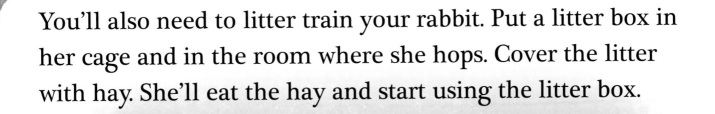

You'll also need to litter train your rabbit. Put a litter box in her cage and in the room where she hops. Cover the litter with hay. She'll eat the hay and start using the litter box.

If you don't train her…

. . . she'll consider the entire cage—and your house—as her personal bathroom!

Your bunny will like chewing on hay.
Give her other chewable things, too.

Mmm . . .
Can't decide which
I love more:
apples or apple
tree branches.

Otherwise...

. . . your bunny's teeth will grow too big.

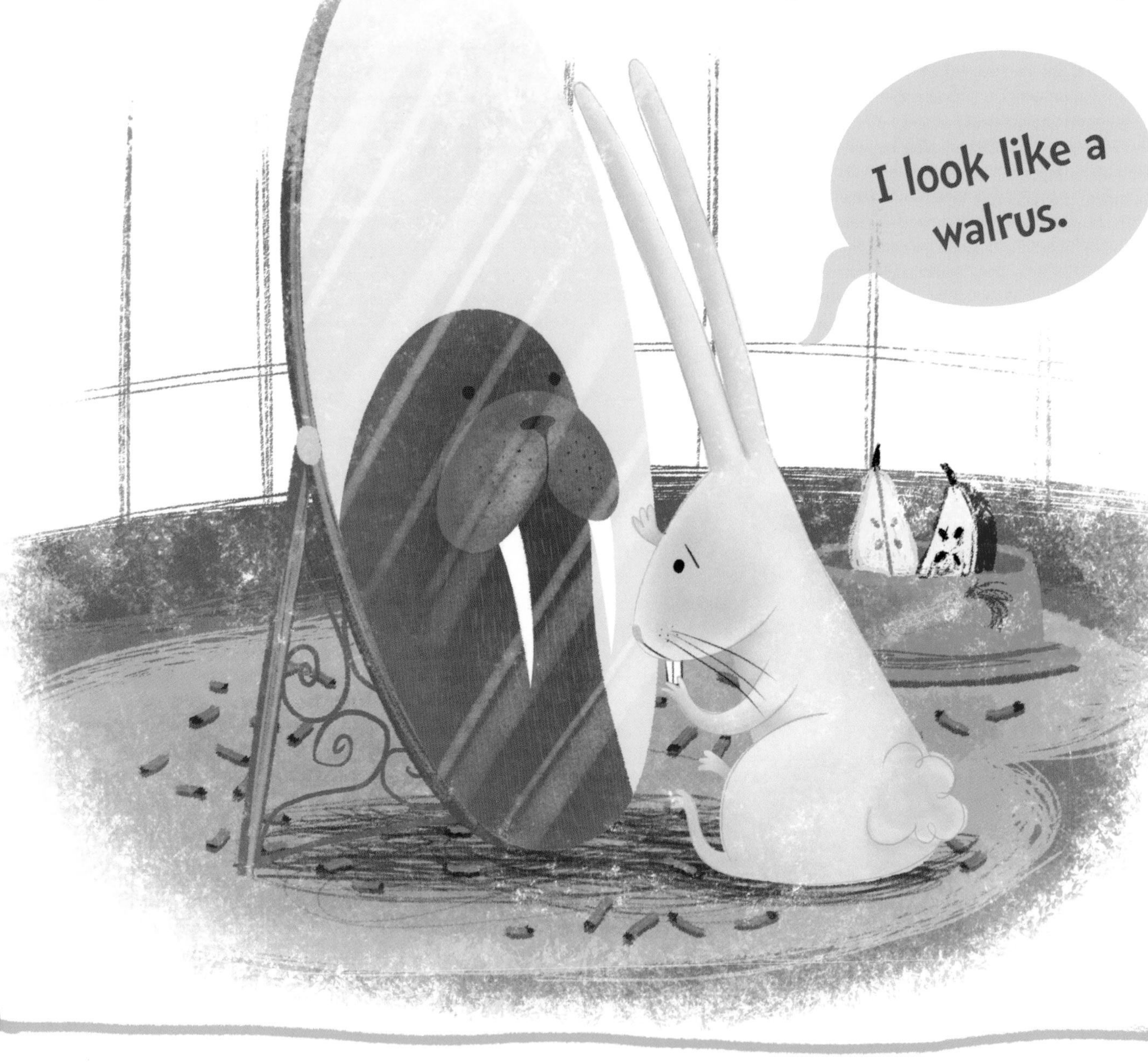

To keep her healthy, feed your rabbit pellets and fresh fruits and veggies. Take her to the vet for checkups. And make sure she gets exercise…

. . . by doing the bunny hop!

When she's out of her cage, keep the door open. She may want to rest . . . or hide. When you leave the house or go to sleep, put her back in her cage.

If you don't…

Watch your rabbit around other pets.
They might become friends . . . or not.

Outside, watch her the whole time. For a pet bunny, even a backyard is dangerous.

At the end of the day, you may hope your bunny will snuggle up with you. Sometimes she will. Other times, she'll prefer her comfy cozy cage. You can still spend time with her.

Rabbits are great listeners . . .
and good friends!

So if you're willing to feed, water, train, and groom her, and keep her safe and her cage clean, then maybe you really do want a rabbit.

Now I have a question for the bunny. You say you want a person. You really, really want a person.

But do you *really* want a person?

Of course you do!

Good bunny, Cupcake!

Good person, Jayla! And good story, Beatrix!

QUIZ

Is this the right pet for me?

What kind of rabbit is right for you? Complete this quiz to find out. (Be sure to talk to breeders, rescue groups, or pet store workers, too!)

1. Do you have room for a large cage?
2. Do you have the time and patience to tame an especially high-strung rabbit?
3. Do you have an hour to groom your pet daily, in addition to training them and letting them exercise?
4. Do you like floppy ears?

If you answered . . .

a. NO TO ONE, you should get a smaller rabbit, also known as a dwarf variety.

b. NO TO TWO, a larger rabbit would be better, as they are calmer.

c. NO TO THREE, you should get a short-haired rabbit.

d. YES TO FOUR, get a lop. They are available in dwarf, giant, long-hair and short- hair varieties.

Websites

ASPCA Kids
http://www.aspca.org/aspcakids.aspx
The American Society for the Prevention of Cruelty
to Animals provides games, photos, and videos that
demonstrate pet care, plus information on careers working
with animals.

House Rabbit Society Rabbit Care Guide
http://www.rabbit.org
The House Rabbit Society is a nonprofit rabbit rescue
organization. Their website provides education on rabbit
care and behavior.

Rabbit Care and Behavior Tips:
The Humane Society of the United States
*http://www.humanesociety.org/animals/rabbits/tips/
rabbit_tips.html*
The Humane Society has advice on bringing a new rabbit
home, feeding, and housing.

Tama and Friends visit Petfinder.com
http://www.petfinder.com/tama//index.html
The kids' section of Petfinder.com offers games, pet tips, pet
listings, and a section for parents.

Read More

Carr, Aaron. *Rabbit.* I Love My Pet.
New York: AV2 by Weigl, 2012.

Harkins, Susan Sales and William H.
Harkins. *Care for a Pet Bunny.* How
to Convince Your Parents You Can—
Hockessin, Del.: Mitchell Lane
Publishers, 2009.

Johnson, Jinny. *Rabbits.* Get to Know
Your Pet. *Mankato, Minn.:* Smart
Apple Media, 2009.

Niven, Felicia Lowenstein. *Learning
to Care for Small Mammals.*
Beginning Pet Care with American
Humane. Berkeley Heights, N.J.:
Bailey Books, 2011.

Sexton, Colleen A. *Caring for Your
Rabbit.* Minneapolis: Bellwether
Media, 2011.

Thump.
Thump.